MW00604334

30 DAYS TO FINANCIAL FITNESS

A Daily Guide to Get Your Finances Right!

by P. M. Tave, MBA

Copyright © 2020 by PeTika Tave

The author and publisher specifically disclaim any responsibility for any liability, loss or risk, personal or otherwise which is incurred as a consequence, either directly or indirectly, by the use and application of any of the contents of this book.

Note: This publication contains the opinions and ideas of its author. It is intended to provide helpful and informative material on the subject matter covered. It is sold with the understanding that the author and publisher are not engaged in rendering professional services in the book. If the reader requires assistance or advice, a competent professional should be consulted.

All rights reserved. This book or parts thereof may not be reproduced in any form, stored in any retrieval system, or transmitted in any form by any means—electronic, mechanical, photocopy, recording, or otherwise—without prior written permission of the publisher, except as provided by United States of America copyright law.

Published by BayaBooks and More
Jacksonville, FL

www.FitMoney101.com
ISBN: 978-1-7341701-2-2
LCCN: 2019920068

DEDICATION

This book is dedicated to my parents, John and Pauletta, my children, Ty and Zee, and everyone else in my financial village that has given me their wise advise and unfiltered opinions.

To mom and dad: You two have always showed me what being responsible and productive looks like. Because of you dad, we have never wanted for anything. You have provided through countless days of laboring and endless nights of being on call. Thank you for teaching me the value of hard work and dedication. Mom, you have ingrained in me the benefits of saving and spending wisely for as far back as I can remember. "Save $25 from each check" served you well and set the stage for me to become a wiser spender and saver through the years.

To Ty and Zee, my reason for all of this: I have worked tirelessly to instill in you the same principles, along with updates, that my parents drilled into me. From being young entrepreneurs to opening your own savings accounts, I hope the lessons I teach lead you to a lifetime of financial security and freedom.

To all the single parents out there: Achieving financial freedom can be done. It may not be easy, and just like anything else, you will encounter setbacks, just persevere, dream big, and hold on to the hope that if you believe it, you can achieve it.

To everyone else looking for financial freedom: This book is made for you too. The principles shared are universal and applies to everyone. Thank you for allowing me to take this journey with you and I look forward to hearing your stories of financial redemption once you complete the steps outlined over the next 30 days.

Be Happy, Live Well!

ABOUT THE AUTHOR

P. M. Tave is a lifelong learner of all things related to personal finance. Growing up in a middle class family, the author was taught many lessons about earning, saving, and giving. What lacked in that education was information about wealth accumulation and investing. After completing three internships in an investment firm and learning about the power of compound interest, P.M. Tave began her journey to become an investing junkie. Vowing to learn everything she could about the topic, Tave went on to pursue a graduate degree in business while maintaining a healthy thirst for knowledge.

Having secured a full-scholarship to attend Florida A&M University, Tave avoided the pitfalls of student loan debt. Nevertheless, a series of financial setbacks during and after college resulted in her filing for bankruptcy and losing her home to foreclosure shortly after the great housing crisis of 2008.

Now, focusing on financial balance and living within her means, Tave has become a role model for single parents, middle-income earners, and countless others on what changes need to be made to live a financially free life.

From owning her own home, raising two kids, living on a teacher's salary, and taking annual family vacations, Tave has accumulated knowledge and expertise, based on her personal experience, that she uses to empower others.

While Tave's methodology includes combining researched best practices with her own understanding, it is critical that no choices be made about your financial future without consulting a licensed professional first.

For more resources and to stay connected with our Financial Fitness community, join us at www.FitMoney101.com.

Earn Money, Live Well!

INTRODUCTION

This book would not be possible if it wasn't for the many financial blunders I have made, despite the wise advice from my mom and dad. From being 21 with over $100,000 in available credit, having almost $60,000 in credit card debt, and eventual bankruptcy, to surviving a foreclosure and raising two children as a single parent, I have learned everything a person should not do if they want to succeed in personal finance.

Ever since I was a high school student completing internships with a powerhouse investment firm, I have inundated myself with knowledge of personal finance. From taking that love of learning to college and earning my Master of Science in Business Administration, to indulging in books from some of the top names in the financial industry, I have been able to get my financial house in order, move towards a debt-free lifestyle, and become a homeowner with a credit score over 800.

Some may question why they should listen to someone that has made the mistakes I have made. I get it, sounds a bit ironic to do so. All I can say is that even with the knowledge I gained early on, youthful exuberance and a few curve balls thrown by life resulted in the financial mess I was in. The principles I am sharing are ones that I should have followed early on and ones that I live by now, which have resulted in my positive turnaround. Experience is often the best teacher, and I since I have endured the biggest financial disasters one can make, learning from my experience can help you get on the path to financial fitness without all the drama and pain.

While I cannot guarantee a successful transition for everyone, I will say that by following the steps in this guide, anyone can get themselves on the path to a stronger, more secure, financial future.

As with anything, the advice provided here is just that, advice. Please consult a financial professional before making decisions that may impact your future.

So, if you're ready to start living a more secure life and want a brighter financial outlook, read and follow the steps in this guide to start your journey to getting financially fit over the next 30 days.

Let's do this!

TABLE OF CONTENTS

Get real about your finances.
It's time to face reality.

To start this journey, it's vital to know where you stand. Like weight loss, it's hard to measure progress without baseline data, or your starting weight. When it comes to financial fitness, you need to understand your current financial situation.

When I came to the realization that I was in over my head with consumer debt, hard decisions had to be made. While facing that reality wasn't easy, it was necessary in order to take control of my financial future.

Answer the following questions to get an idea of where you are today:

1. What is your total household income?
2. What kind of debt do you have (i.e., credit card, car loans, mortgage, personal loans)?
3. How much debt do you have (i.e., How much do you owe – roughly)?
4. Do you have any savings (i.e., an emergency fund)?
5. What have you saved for retirement?
6. Do you have a will?
7. Do you have a power of attorney?
8. Are you happy with your finances?
9. What is your biggest financial goal?
10. What are your biggest financial barriers?

Answering these questions should get you thinking about your current financial situation. When done with this step, you can start to devise a financial plan. Use the space below to summarize your current financial state.

_____
_____
_____
_____
_____
_____

Now that you have taken a good look at your financial situation, it's time to make a decision. Just like committing to get physically fit, getting your financial house in order is more of a mental exercise than a physical one. Let me explain. The human mind is a brilliant specimen. When a person sets their mind on achieving a goal, very little can stop them. From losing 50 pounds to paying off $50,000 in debt, changing one's mindset is a surefire way to reach a goal.

So how do you commit to get financially fit? You've already completed the first step – knowing where you stand. Now that the reality of your situation is front and center, you've got to decide if completing your financial goal is worth the effort it will take.

Let me be clear. The concept is simple. It's the follow through where people stumble the most. The best way to solidify your commitment to financial fitness is to do the following:

1. Create a list that describes why you want to improve your financial situation.

2. Think about possible road blocks that may stand in your way. Write them down.

3. Pick a day that you will start your journey. Be sure it's soon so you don't stop before you even start.

4. Create a mantra or phrase you'll say to remind yourself of why you need to stay the course. You'll need to remember and recite it throughout this journey.

Example: "I can and will be financially fit by January 2021."

Use the space below to complete today's steps:

_____
_____
_____
_____
_____
_____
_____
_____
_____

Any great financial fitness program has to include taking a look at your credit. This may be a gut-wrenching experience for some, but it must be done. Why, you ask? Credit is how consumers borrow money. Although some may be blessed with the ability to pay cash for major purchases, many people need good credit to buy a house or a car, get a job, and even for competitive insurance rates. It's truly a necessary evil to enjoy some of the essentials of life.

As with anything, before you can fix a problem, you have to face it head on. While my credit score has been mostly respectable, at one point it dipped down to the 630s. I knew I could do better. Assessing my financial situation was the first step in moving towards an excellent credit rating. Today I want you to face your credit so that you can confidently move forward with this 30-day plan.

Follow the steps below to stop being afraid of your credit and start building a solid reputation for paying off debt:

1. Get a copy of your credit report from all three bureaus. You can go to www.annualcreditreport.com to get them for free.

2. Check each credit report for inaccuracies. Look for the following:

   a. Fraudulent charges

   b. Inaccurate reporting

   c. Open accounts (Make sure the payment history is correct.)

   d. Closed accounts (Make sure they are at $0 balance and were reported correctly.)

3. Determine how much debt is listed on your credit report. This is the stepping stone to paying off old debts that may be weighing you down.

4. Order your FICO credit score. The goal is for it to be at least 700. Ultimately, having a score over 760 means you have excellent credit, but you need to start somewhere.

Once you have completed these steps, you are miles ahead of where you used to be financially. After facing your credit, make a plan to fix it as soon as possible. How to go about doing that begins with tomorrow's task.

Make notes about your credit below. Include any inaccuracies, companies to contact, or questions you need answered:

Now that you are aware of your financial situation and are committed to fixing it, it's time to dig deeper by determining all of your debt. On day one you tallied a rough estimate of it. That's great! Today you'll take a look at the outstanding balances and due dates. When done, you'll be ready to develop a plan to pay them off. For now, don't be concerned with the interest rates of the debt because you'll use a simple payoff strategy to tackle that monster.

The most effective debt reduction strategy I like to use requires that you pay off your smallest debt first. How? First, pay the minimum amount due on **all** balances owed. Then, use any extra money you have left to add on to the smallest debt balance. Once you pay the smallest debt off, take the money you were paying on it then add it to the minimum payment for the next smallest debt to knock that one out. When done, take *that* money and add it to the amount you pay the new smallest debt. Continue the pattern until all debts are paid off. Depending on your total outstanding debt, this can take a few months to a few years.

This step is essential in getting your finances straight. Use the space below to start laying out what you owe:

- Major Credit Cards

- Store Cards

- Bank Loans

- Car Loans

- Personal Loans

- Student Loans

- Other Debt Payments/Loans

Mortgage Loan – For the purpose of the simple debt reduction method, we ignore the mortgage loan at this time. The concern for this step is to get rid of unnecessary consumer debt. While a mortgage is a debt, it's necessary to have a place to live. That is why it's excluded.

Get your **mind** right.

Prepare for positive changes.

Set S.M.A.R.T. Goals

Do you want to be a millionaire? Multi-millionaire? Debt free? Financially stable? Earn passive income? All of these are a possibility when a clear goal is set and a concrete plan is made to achieve them.

For example, I want to run a 5K in less than 40 minutes by training and improving my eating habits within the next four months, is a very specific goal that is also S.M.A.R.T. – specific, measurable, achievable, relevant, and time-constrained. You'll need a goal like that to get on the path to financial fitness.

Today's task is to think about what you want your finances to look like in three months, six months, one year, and five years. Based on that vision, I want you to choose a short-term and long-term goal you wish to accomplish. Brainstorm on a separate sheet of paper and write the results below. After that, post your new S.M.A.R.T. goals on your mirror, or somewhere visible, so that you are reminded of what you're working towards each day.

Short-Term S.M.A.R.T. Goal (less than a year):

Specific: _____

Measurable: _____

Attainable/Reasonable: _____

Relevant: _____

Time constrained: _____

Complete goal stated in a sentence: _____

_____

Long-Term S.M.A.R.T. Goal (1-5 years):

Specific: _____

Measurable: _____

Attainable/Reasonable: _____

Relevant: _____

Time constrained: _____

Complete goal stated in a sentence: _____

_____

Create Your "Smart Money" Village

Many people say that it takes a village to raise a child, but when that child grows up, if they haven't been taught the fundamentals of personal finance, which is often the case, who is responsible for teaching them then? It's time to stop avoiding financial talks and get empowered with knowledge. One surefire way to do that, short of learning from your parents, is to build a "smart money" village.

A "smart money" village is a group of people that you feel comfortable getting open and honest with about your money. It should be made up of like-minded individuals who share the same or similar beliefs as you do about cash. Or, if you've been living a "wine life" on a "beer budget," your village may consist of people that are already where you want to be financially.

Think of your village as a group of mentors working for a common cause – to increase financial literacy and personal wealth to become (or remain) financially free.

To create your village, do the following:

1. Think of siblings, cousins, parents, grandparents, aunts, uncles, and co-workers that are where you want to be financially.

2. Seek out people of different backgrounds, cultures, and age ranges who are willing to join the village and share experiences that will empower and educate you.

3. Look for social media groups and meetups that you can join so that even if you can't have a "smart money" village of people you know, you can still be inspired by people that will push you in the right direction. Try our group on Facebook, SingleParentSaves. It's open to all.

Next, ask yourself:

1. Can I be open and honest with my smart money villagers?

2. Do they have knowledge I can benefit from and vice versa?

3. Do I trust their input and care about what they say – judgment free?

Once you have created a list of possible candidates, it's time to recruit people to help you get on the path to financial freedom. Write down the people you'd like to invite below then reach out to them. Be honest. Tell them what you want, how they can help, and how it can be a mutually beneficial relationship. You might be surprised with the results. Who knows, they may be looking for the same accountability!

Who to Invite	Contact Information	Result of Contact

Contrary to popular belief, you don't need to pay hundreds of dollars to some strange company in order to fix your credit. Let's be clear. Nobody, I repeat, NOBODY, can erase negative items off your credit report if it's rightfully there.

When you use credit to buy things, you have borrowed money and made a promise to pay it back. Just as if you loaned money out to others, they also expect repayment of what was given, plus interest. If you don't uphold your part of the deal, they have every right to go after you for what you owe. Makes sense, right?

With that in mind, the following are actions I suggest to fix your credit. They are simple and straightforward so you can do them by yourself. Although I filed for bankruptcy because I was truly unable to pay my bills, I used these methods before I had to cave in. If you can maintain for just a bit without filing bankruptcy, I highly recommend it. It took 10 years to get to the credit rating I have today.

The best way to fix your credit is to pay off your debt. When you get your credit reports, you need to go through each one and verify what's on them. Once you do that, take steps to arrange a settlement of debts less than seven years old, start a history of on-time payments for current debt, then work your way towards a cash-only lifestyle.

Follow the steps below to start fixing your credit:

1. Verify that all debts on your credit reports are yours. This is important to make sure there are no fraudulent transactions on it and to add the correct balances to your budget.

2. Check to see if there is anything reported as outstanding that should be removed from your account because it was paid as agreed and not correctly listed.

3. List the negative accounts on your reports and work out a settlement with each company to pay them off for a fraction of the cost. Aim for $.20 for every dollar. (Note: DO NOT agree to pay off debts older than seven years and DO NOT send any money without a settlement amount from the company made in writing.)

4. Once the companies have agreed in writing to a settlement amount, send the payment in full and check back in a few months to make sure

the item is removed from your report, or add it to your budget, per the repayment agreement.

5. Do that process for every debt to clean up your reports. (Note: You'll have to do this for each credit report since there may be different information on each version.)

Pay all current debts on time until they are paid off. Once all debt is paid, move towards a cash-only lifestyle.

Sounds complicated? Maybe. Is it doable? Absolutely. As you go through each credit report, complete the above steps. You'll feel so free when you're done!

DAY 8 — Pay Yourself First

One of the biggest mistakes people make is forgetting to pay themselves first. Yes, I said it. You need to pay yourself FIRST! Key items in your budget should include saving for retirement and emergencies. Many financial gurus vary on their advice as to when to start paying yourself, but they all agree that you must save for yourself sooner rather than later.

Some say take 10 percent of every check and save as soon as you start working. Others say pay off your debts first then stash away cash for the future. The choice is yours as to what you ultimately decide, but I tend to stick to the thought that the longer you are able to save, the more your money grows, meaning that I chose to save for my future and knock out debt at the same time.

Paying yourself first could start out as saving one percent of each check. The key is getting into the habit of making regular contributions to your future. Think of it like this - we all plan to live to a ripe old age, so how would the 70-year-old version of you feel if you had to keep working because you spent all of your cash when you were younger? Not a thrilling thought, huh?

As you pay off your debts, you'll be able to increase the contributions to yourself until you have three to six months of an emergency fund and are allocating 15 percent of your income to retirement. This is the true key to becoming financially fit, so it's not something you should delay or skimp on.

Here's another perspective: Americans log over 40 hours a week or 8+ hours a day, just to see all that money bleed out of their checking accounts to pay bills. Why endure 12 years of mandatory school and four or more years of college, then pay thousands of dollars in student loan debt, just to send your entire paycheck to someone else every pay period?

When you pay yourself first, you are saving for your future, sanity, retirement, vacations, and anything else you want. Unless you embarked on a career to let others reap the benefits of your talent and energy, saving for yourself is like paying yourself for your time and efforts. You deserve it!

I pay myself by saving for retirement, having an emergency fund, saving for self-care, family vacations, and the occasional splurge. Even when embarking on a debt reduction plan, you should make yourself a priority.

So, if you haven't done so already, tomorrow you will learn how to add yourself to the budget. Hence, the task for today is to think about reasons to start paying yourself FIRST!

The journey continues.
It's time to take action!

Tell Your Money Where to Go
(a.k.a. create a budget)

You should be feeling really awesome by now. Go ahead, pat yourself on the back. With a S.M.A.R.T. goal in place and a village of financial cheerleaders on your side, it's time to create a budget that tells every dollar that enters your bank account where to go.

Please don't get caught up in the hype of hating budgets. Remember, budgets are your friends. They help you get a grip on your finances by knowing exactly how much income you have and deciding where it all should go.

In fact, that's exactly what budgeting does. It's not meant to be a tool that limits your ability to enjoy life. The purpose is to take control of your money so that you *can* enjoy life. Now that we have that clear, it's time to get started on creating your budget.

While there are many budgeting tools, software, and spreadsheets available (see our website), follow these simple strategies to get started on yours right now:

1. Make a list of everything you need to pay each month – yourself, mortgage/rent, insurance, gas, hair care, daycare expenses, cable, cell phone, internet, everything!

2. Once you have that down, write the monthly cost for each one. You may wish to look at your banking history for the past three months to calculate an average.

3. Next, determine how much steady income you receive each month. Unless absolutely necessary, I wouldn't recommend adding child support to this number, especially if it's inconsistent. The goal is to live off of what *you* earn.

4. If you get paid bi-weekly, decide how much you need to set aside from each check to cover the monthly cost of all your bills. If you get paid once a month, you should be fine.

5. I would highly recommend adding categories for sinking funds, such as gifts, irregular expenses, and car maintenance. This will help you set aside cash so that when those bills arrive, you'll have the money to cover them. (Learn more about this on Day 10.)

6. Finally, make your budget. I like to use a spreadsheet (see our FitMoney101 website), but if a spreadsheet is not your cup of tea, use a budget app to create one. There are tons of great apps that will even

When doing your budget, tell every penny where to go. Don't leave anything to chance! Budget for everything so no dollar is spent on a whim. In fact, create a line item for "fun" if you have any cash left after taking care of all of your savings and obligations. You earned it, so you should treat yourself to something each paycheck, even if it's a small ice cream cone at the end of each month. Now go create your budget!

Create Sinking Funds

Yesterday's task resulted in the creation of a budget, a way for you to take control of your cash and know where every penny goes. To make a budget truly beneficial, you need to open sinking funds for some of your spending categories.

By now you may be asking, "What is a sinking fund?" Simply put, a sinking fund is a savings account created to cover expenses that you know will come up each year. You contribute to these dedicated accounts every pay day with the expectation that when the expense is due, it is already funded.

Sinking funds are a wonderful savings strategy because you always have the cash needed for a specific expense. For example, when it's time to buy new clothes, you don't have to cringe about spending money since it's already available. Similarly, when it's time to give gifts, just withdraw what's needed from your sinking fund for gifts, and voila! No stress. No worries.

You can create sinking funds for anything. The possibilities are endless! Think of expenses that must be paid and create an account for each of them. For example, I have funds for the following. You may want to consider them, too:

1. Family Vacation
2. Car Insurance
3. Personal Care/Self-Care
4. Car Repairs and Maintenance
5. Summer Camp
6. Gifts
7. Kids – Field Trips/Yearbooks/Incidentals
8. Clothes
9. Emergencies
10. Home repairs and maintenance

For people seeking financial fitness, sinking funds are game changers. It certainly works for me. It's such a simple concept that has tremendous benefits. Once they are set up, there's not much else to do except fund them. So go out and open a few sinking funds today!

Many banks, especially credit unions, allow you to open multiple savings accounts with as little as $5. Once opened, name each account for its intended purpose. Then, set up automatic deposits based on what you need to save each month, which you calculated in your budget. For example, you may allocate the following:

- Summer camp fund - $50 per month

- Personal self-care fund - $50 per month

- Gift fund - $25 per month

For people seeking financial fitness, sinking funds are game changers. It certainly works for me. It's such a simple concept that has tremendous benefits. Once they are set up, there's not much else to do except fund them. So go out and open a few sinking funds today!

You are rocking and rolling superstar! You've managed to power through a little over a week of financial fitness and look at some of what you've accomplished:

- Facing your financial situation
- Assessing your debt
- Recruiting help through your "smart money" village
- Setting S.M.A.R.T. goals
- Creating a budget
- Setting up sinking funds

All of this is wonderful! So go ahead, take a moment to look in the mirror and congratulate yourself for making progress. You're a lot further along than you would have been had you not started.

Today's task is fairly simple. Now that you have a budget and have opened sinking funds, it's time to put your plan on autopilot.

Creating sinking funds is easy enough. The way to really make them work is to "set it and forget it" by automating deposits. Using your primary checking account, or the account where your direct deposit from work enters, you need to set up automatic payments to each of your debts and sinking funds based on your budget.

Think of it this way. If you get paid on Thursdays, your funds will arrive into your primary account every pay day. Once you set up automatic transactions, you can decide that on Friday your money will leave your account and end up where it needs to go.

Visualize this. All of your money goes into a large pot, like soup. When it's time to be distributed, or served, a robot takes portions out of the pot and places it into individual bowls. That's what your bank will do.

Since you know how much you need to take from each check to pay bills and build your sinking funds, it's now time to set up bill pay and automatic withdrawals to truly accelerate your financial fitness plan. When you set everything up, your money really does have a place to go and will head there on its own after every pay period. Fascinating!

With that, go to your bank and set up your automatic transactions. The few minutes you spend getting that done today will lead to many unbelievably stress free nights. So go ahead, do it!

Take a deep breath.
You're doing great!

Spend Wisely

Holidays, birthdays, happy days, stress-filled days - any day is a great day to spend! Or is it? Oftentimes, people can think of any number of ways to waste unbelievable amounts of money. Even if you're frugal, spending $10 here and $20 there quickly adds up. In fact, I once knew a family of three – an adult, teen, and child – that spent almost $700 on groceries in one month! Insanity!

Today's task is to learn to spend wisely and make smarter choices. Now that you have a budget and predetermined amounts of money going to sinking funds, it's important to make sure that your expenditures are within reason and are not done on impulse. We're all guilty of it, but it's time to put an end to it. Today!

Take a moment to complete the questions below to make sure that you are aware of your triggers and can start spending wisely.

1. What do you spend the most on? (i.e., food, clothes, entertainment)

_____

_____

2. When do you usually go shopping? (i.e., on a whim, with friends, weekends, with kids, on your own)

_____

_____

3. What are your spending triggers? (i.e., boredom, anxiety, fear, joy, sadness, stress)

_____

_____

4. What can you do when the urge to spend emerges?

_____

_____

5. Who can you call if you are about to go on a spending spree to help you stop?

_____

_____

While curbing your spending is a definitive way to have more control over your cash, the truth is that there are daily necessities that we all must buy. Even small repetitive purchases can quickly add up. Relax though. Finding ways to save is within reach, requiring minimal effort for maximum results.

Now I am not one to coupon, it requires a lot of time and planning. And to be quite frank, no one ever made the millionaires list by spending hours creating binders, buying newspapers, and chasing sales. You can use that time a bit more efficiently, in my opinion. That's not to say that the occasional coupon that comes in the mail for toiletries is not useful. Just don't spend hours on blog sites and in groups trying to save a few dollars. Yes, savings can add up, just not that fast.

So what are some easy savings hacks you can use that will deliver maximum results? Actually they're quite simple, and some of them you have already completed. Read on:

- **Hack 1: Make a budget and stick to it.**

  The benefits of a budget cannot be emphasized enough. If you have a budget, or a plan for every dollar you get, you have control over how it's spent and where it goes. This gives you power, confidence, and motivation to stay on the road to financial fitness.

- **Hack 2: Buy store brands.**

  Store brands used to get a bad rap. However, now that the secret is out about the difference between store and name brands - they are usually manufactured by the same company in the same facility - you can choose to save a little cash instead of wasting it. Buying store brands will save you thousands over your lifetime and make for a much heftier bank account.

- **Hack 3: Plan your meals.**

  Buying groceries is often the most expensive discretionary item in one's budget. Eating out compounds the damage. The easiest savings hack you can choose is to plan your meals and eat at home. That's it!

All of these seem painless, right? They are. Revisit Day 1 to see what your biggest expenditures are. Next, check your budget to see what you have allocated to discretionary expenses. Now go online and search one of those items, along with the words "savings hacks," to learn even more ways to save. For example, if you need to reduce car insurance, search "car insurance savings hacks." Look through some of the results and decide what's easiest for you.

Write one thing you'll search to find savings hacks:

_____

_____

Save on Groceries

Ever felt like groceries are eating away at your savings (pun intended)? The family mentioned in Day 12 who spent nearly $700 on groceries in one month was mine! And the month it happened in was February, the shortest month of the year! How is that even possible?!

I'll tell you how. Our family has an affinity for gourmet food from gourmet places. But I'm not talking about eating out. From fresh bread, sparkling grape juice, wine, and exotic dishes to premium cheeses and fancy desserts, I can show you how reckless spending on groceries can really derail your finances.

That's why, just like anything else, it's important to enjoy what you love, but within reason. Eating healthy, or fancy for that matter, doesn't have to be a financial grave digger if you know how to find ways to save on groceries.

The following are a few tips to master your grocery budget while enjoying your favorites:

1. **Set up a sinking fund for groceries based on your average monthly needs.** Then decide how often you'll take shopping trips – weekly, bi-weekly, daily, or as needed.

2. **Pay for groceries using only cash.** That's right, just cash! Once you run out, don't buy anything else until the grocery fund is replenished by your next check. This is essential!

3. **Create a grocery list and stick to it.** I like to put little boxes next to each item so that I can check them off as I grab them. Also, estimate the cost of groceries by writing the price of the item next to it on the list. This allows you to prioritize and have an idea of how much you'll spend.

4. **Avoid packaged foods.** They are usually processed and are not very healthy. Stick to things that occur naturally – either from a plant or an animal.

5. **Save even more by buying fruits and vegetables in season.** It's critical.

6. **Serve water as a drink.** You can infuse it with fruit and veggies or drink it plain. This eliminates sugary drinks and cuts the cost of high calorie juices and sodas.

7. **Use leftovers to make new meals.** If your family doesn't mind, serve leftover dinner for lunch the next day as well. This really helps.

8. **Allow for a new food item on each shopping trip.** Some foods are seasonal, so they are only available for a limited time. In life, it's important to spice things up and have new experiences. This goes for food too, so make sure to try something new so that you won't feel deprived.

That's it! Easy right? Following these tips can help you get grocery spending under control. Using coupons can help too, but if fresh foods make up the bulk of your list, they won't do much. At any rate, put the tips above into practice and you'll start saving tons on groceries in no time!

By now you're feeling one of two ways – relieved that you have come this far, visualizing a wonderful financial future, or relieved by what you have done but overwhelmed by it all. Either way is fine. As one famous proverb states, "The journey of a thousand miles begins with a single step," so your road to financial fitness started with you facing your finances and getting a grip on reality. While you've made it to this point and still may have quite a journey ahead, you are a lot further than you were 15 days ago. For that, give yourself some kudos. It's time for a bit of celebration.

Like with anything else, it's easy to experience burnout when you get so entrenched in an activity that it begins to define you. The purpose of this book is not to stress you out, rather, to give you daily goals that move you closer to financial freedom. With that in mind, incorporate the following tips to avoid financial burnout:

1. Think about the goals you've set for your financial future. They will help you persevere.

2. Celebrate the progress you've made in gaining financial awareness and taking steps to become financially fit.

3. Check in with your village at least once a month, maybe even weekly when starting, to share your progress and push through difficult days.

4. Have a plan to deal with stress so that you avoid compulsive spending or emotional shopping.

5. Give thanks. Write down three things you are thankful for below. Go ahead, think of three.

    a. _____

    b. _____

    c. _____

6. Aim to show gratitude at least weekly. Either write what you are thankful for in a gratitude journal or look in the mirror and remind yourself of everything you are happy about.

7. Do something fun that doesn't cost anything. Take a walk, go to the beach, read a great book. Just relax.

8. Keep everything in perspective. There will be times when you'll want to give up. Resist them. Stay encouraged and grounded. You may not be perfect all the time, but what you are doing is making positive steps towards your financial future.

Keep moving forward.

No regrets.

A key trait of financially fit individuals is having a solid foundation in financial literacy. Financial literacy is the ability to understand how money works. It is also defined as having the set of skills and knowledge that allows an individual to make informed and effective decisions with all of their financial resources.

As mentioned earlier, I started learning about financial literacy while interning during high school. That love of knowledge never left, and to this day you can find me relaxing with a cup of coffee (home-brewed, of course), sitting in a chair and reading the latest financial literature. It's addictive.

In order to become financially literate, you must educate yourself too. Not in the sense of attending school for a formal lesson, but constantly reading and learning to better equip yourself with the knowledge needed to make sound financial decisions.

While there are countless financial gurus with their own spin on financial "dos and don'ts," the core of their information is the same. Consult with your village to find out their favorite mentors and book titles. You can also visit our online community at www.FitMoney101.com to share ideas and get the latest information that will make you more comfortable with your finances in no time. Do a little research or call a friend today. Then, grab a copy of their recommended book from your local library to start your journey to financial literacy.

What books have been recommended to you?

_____

Which book do you think you'll read first?

_____

When will you get the book?

_____

What day will you start reading it?

_____

OK, so it's been just over two weeks since you've started your journey and lots of progress has been made. While the momentum of getting in financial control is what got you going, it's around this time that energy starts to wane and you need a quick boost to stay on course. Today is great day to check in with your village.

Scroll back to day six and revisit the people you identified as accountability partners. Whether they are trusted family members or online friends, making contact and sharing your thoughts will help you manage any negative feelings that may start to creep in.

Perhaps there are a few questions you need answered, some advice you'd like to receive, or a decision that you'd like a second opinion on. Don't be afraid to reach out. That's what your village is for!

If you're in a good space and feeling great, share that too! Your village would love to hear both the positives and negatives of your journey. It'll be the boost they need to keep them encouraged as well as offer you more mojo as you power through the next two weeks. So take a few moments to check in with your village. Don't forget to visit us online as well. Use the space below to organize any questions you have or progress you want to share.

Let your village be a part of this journey!

Sometimes in order to get financially fit you simply need to earn more cash. There are two ways to do that. You can either change careers and get paid your worth or work a side job until you are out of debt.

While this may seem like a daunting task, it really isn't. Earning extra cash may require you to monetize a hobby or skill that you enjoy. Many people like to call this a side hustle. Now it's easy to get caught up in the typically advertised money making schemes – taking surveys, using cash back apps, and dog-walking – but you really have to decide what you can do, want to do, need to do, and will do.

What *can* you do?

List a few skills and talents that you have. Singing, dancing, decorating, organizing, cleaning. This is the starting point for your side hustle.

What do you *want* to do?

What brings joy to your heart, or at least what are you able to do? A few ideas include pet sitting, delivering food, babysitting, doing small tasks for other people, and creating crafts.

What *will* you do?

Can you teach online? Will you walk dogs, style hair, sell products, work for app-based companies, or do ride sharing? Is there anything you won't do?

Once you have answered these questions, you can narrow down your options. Make a list of possible jobs that interest you and go out there and make some more money!

Plan ahead.
Your future depends on it.

In order to be ready for the long term, it's critical to contribute to retirement savings. This topic either gets people excited about the possibilities or grumpy over the fact that saving for retirement is a MUST!

Think about it. If you plan to live well into your 80s and don't want to be forced to work until you take your last breath, saving for retirement is not optional, it's a requirement, and the sooner you start, the better off you'll be.

To begin, you need to determine if you have a retirement account. Check with your employer to see if you're contributing to a 401K or 403B. If not, it's time to begin, but we'll discuss that later. You may also need to find out if you have a ROTH IRA or a Traditional IRA. You wouldn't have both because they are income dependent.

Once you know what you have, it's important to check its balance and where you're invested. It may be necessary to sit with a financial planner to evaluate your current holdings and performance. After that is done, develop a strategy for future contributions and aim to add 15 percent of your income to it each month. Better yet, automate it so that you can set it and forget it. Trust me, you won't regret it when it's time to kick back, relax, and enjoy your golden years.

While this is an extremely watered down version of what really needs to happen when it comes to a retirement check-up, it is absolutely necessary.

If you already have retirement accounts and are contributing 15 percent, look at its growth over the past few years and remind yourself why this is important. Be thankful that you are taking control of your financial future and aim to learn a little more about investing to understand what's happening to your money even more.

Account Type	Account Holder	Current Balance	Annual Contributions
ROTH IRA	Bing Bank	$56,000	15%
403B	AquaMax	$25,467	5%

Ramp Up Your Contributions

Now that you have a clear picture of your retirement accounts, it's time to ramp up your contributions.

No matter how much you plan to save for retirement, a great target amount for regular contributions is 15 percent of your income, starting as soon (young) as possible. You'll want to keep it at a percentage of income so as your salary increases through the years, your contributions will too.

One thing to note is that anything over 15 percent is completely optional, but if your company has matches, that percent does not count for your total. In other words, 15 percent is a measure of the contributions you make, not your company. Any extra they add is a nice boost. Also, you don't need to add 15 percent to each account you have, rather your total contributions should add up to that amount.

Some financial advisors recommend that you pay off debt before starting contributions while others believe the power of compound interest is too great to ignore and that you should make regular contributions as soon as you start working. It's up to you to decide what route to take. Get started now, boost deposits to 15 percent of your income, then automate the withdrawals so you can set it and forget it.

Next steps:

1. Determine the total amount of retirement contributions you currently make each year and what percentage of your income that is. (Divide your total contributions by your salary.)

2. Decide how much you need to add to your contributions to reach 15 percent, or if you're already contributing 15 percent, determine if you need to reallocate funds.

3. Make the changes necessary to reach your savings goals by setting up direct deposits into each retirement account.

Notes:

1. Common wisdom is to contribute up to your company's match (if offered) in a 401K then place anything else in a ROTH IRA.

2. Use an online retirement calculator to make sure you are saving enough money to meet your retirement needs. You can do a simple check via any online search engine.

Make any notes you need to complete this step below:

To make sure the changes you've made are working properly, it's time to do a quick checkup of your finances. Sometimes when you start on a course to accomplish a goal, the brain begins a firestorm of ideas that opens your eyes and gets you excited to do even more.

Today's activity encourages you to listen to the voice in your head that is churning with ideas about how to advance this journey even further, because now you're completely invested in your financial fitness plan.

Tackle a few of the questions below to make sure you are on track to reach your goals:

1. Were there or are there any surprises about your finances?

2. Are you doing better or worse than you thought?

3. Do you need to make any adjustments to your financial fitness plan?

4. What challenges may come up with sticking to your plan?

5. What can you do to handle those challenges effectively?

6. Has your commitment to becoming financially fit increased or decreased in the last 21 days? Explain.

It's the little things that make
the biggest impact.

Stay focused.

Get a Tax Checkup

Although many people live for their coveted tax refund check, getting a bonus in the spring isn't exactly good business. The goal of every individual should be to neither pay or owe taxes come tax time. If you typically get a large refund, you may need to adjust your withholding. If you owe money each year, it's definitely time to get a tax checkup.

I realize that some people may argue that getting a refund is a way to feel good when tax season arrives. It's like a bonus! In some cases, a combination of credits and deductions may qualify the person for a refund of all monies paid plus some. Nice, right? Not so fast.

If the refund measures in the thousands, you've probably overpaid. How so? Simply put, you are allowing the IRS to take too much money out of your check. The purpose of tax deductions each pay period is to make sure you pay Uncle Sam only what you owe him, nothing more.

If you find that you get a large refund every year, you need to reduce how much is deducted from your checks. Why? Because the more money you bring home each pay period, the more buying power you have throughout the year. It's better to get your cash now than in a few months.

On the flip side, if you constantly owe money, you may need to increase your payments. You can easily change your withholding to deduct more from each check. This allows you to spread your tax liability over time to avoid a large bill in April.

Before making any of these changes you should consult a tax professional for individualized advice. If you want to handle it on your own, go to the online calculator at www.irs.gov to see suggested deductions based on current tax law. Once you have that information, contact your employer and update your W-4. That's it! Piece of cake, huh?

Shore Up Your Emergency Fund

When it comes to emergencies, one thing is certain, they WILL arise. The question is do you have the cash to cover one. With your financial fitness plan in full swing, it is critical to your future health that you avoid using credit cards. They only keep you in debt. When emergencies creep up, you want to have an emergency fund in place that you can rely on to draw from, guilt-free.

Early in your journey you should have created a sinking fund for emergencies. Now the goal is to ramp it up to at least $1000, with the ultimate goal of having three to six months of expenses saved after all your consumer debt is paid off.

What is an emergency fund used for?

Emergency funds are for just that, emergencies. A clogged toilet, slow moving drains, car repairs, HVAC system failures, and the dreaded job loss are a few. The point is that if you are prepared for whatever curve ball life throws you, you'll walk away with little more than a few bumps and bruises to your financial fitness plan. You'll be able to quickly recover by replenishing your money supply.

What do you need to do?

Revisit your sinking fund for emergencies. What is the current balance? How much are you contributing to it? Can you add more so that you can reach $1000 in the next six to twelve months? If you can save it faster, do that. It'll make you feel 100 percent better knowing you have that cushion in place. It surely helped me when my HVAC unit went berserk!

Fill in the spaces below to determine your next steps:

1. What is the total balance in your emergency fund?

_____

_____

2. Can you add more each pay period?

_____

_____

3. When do you expect to pay off your debt?

_____

_____

4. How much money do you need to save for three months of expenses?

_____

_____

5. How long will it take you to save that amount after your debts are paid off?

_____

_____

6. What's the total amount of time it will take to pay off your debt and save three months of emergency money?

_____

_____

DAY 24

Ignore the Joneses

People are consumed with the idea of the American dream. Big house, nice cars, designer clothes, manicured yards, Ivy League kids, the list goes on and on! But if that isn't enough, in order to truly be on top, some feel that they have to "one up" their friends, family, and/or neighbors. This leads to the symbolic Jones family that people try to keep up with.

The Jones family tends to be the one driving the latest high-end car and wearing the best brands of clothes. They have picture-perfect kids that are scholars and/or athletes, and they are the epitome of wealth. Having an excellent career and living in an exclusive neighborhood makes them the envy of family and so-called friends. Since they are among the elites, even their neighbors feel the need to compete with them. Vacationing is a right. Exotic locations are a must. The more elaborate their parties, the more people tend to grovel at their feet.

While none of that sounds like a life to relish, sadly it's what many compare themselves to. The Jones family is the perceived goal among all income levels. Simply put, it means there is a middle-class Jones family, a lower-class one, and an upper-class one.

Your job today is to avoid focusing on what other people have and to take pleasure in simplicity. Show gratitude for your accomplishments in life. Look for the good in every situation, even the less than desirable ones. Find joy in experiences that create memories rather than things that decrease in value. In a nutshell, ignore the Joneses.

1. What are you most proud of?

_____

_____

2. What do you want to achieve the most?

_____

_____

3. Why do you want that?

_____

_____

Keep moving.
You're almost there!

Insurance is a practice or arrangement by which a company or government agency provides a guarantee of compensation for specified loss, damage, illness, or death in return for payment of a premium. Everyone loves to hate it, but you won't appreciate how much you need it until you do. Even if the thought of insurance makes you shudder, it's important to protect yourself and get insured.

People need insurance for everything – cars, health, home, life, disability. Insurance helps make sure that you are covered in the event of the unexpected. It's also one of those things you pay for that you hope you never have to use. Yes, that's contrary to what we are raised to believe, but if you have to use car insurance, you probably got into an accident. Tapping into health insurance can mean you're taking advantage of preventative care or that you've encountered a major medical issue that requires attention. If you use your home or disability insurance, something catastrophic must have happened, and if your family cashes in on life insurance, someone they love is not around to enjoy it.

In all of those situations, the miniscule amounts of premiums you pay provides a buffer in the event of a major financial event. This is why having adequate, and the right kind of insurance, is a necessity to achieve financial fitness.

Honestly, what you need to have includes all the types listed above. I wouldn't recommend other things, such as cancer riders, but you should contact your financial advisor or estate planner to determine what's best for you.

To begin having insurance related conversations, it's important to know what policies you have, their payouts, your beneficiaries, and any details that may aide in making decisions about them. Once you have an idea about your current insurance status, you should take steps to make sure you are properly protected in any situation.

1. Do you have the following insurance?

     O   Life   O   Home   O   Disability

     O   Medical   O   Life

2. Does each policy have a beneficiary?

3. If you don't have a policy, who will you call to inquire about one?

4. What do you want from your insurance?

5. What questions do you have about insurance?

_____
_____
_____
_____
_____
_____
_____
_____
_____
_____
_____
_____
_____
_____
_____
_____
_____
_____
_____
_____
_____
_____
_____
_____
_____
_____
_____
_____
_____
_____

One of the last few components of financial fitness that this book will address is getting your legal house in order. What's the point in getting financially fit if the court system will decide what happens to your estate if you pass on without proper planning? Absolutely none. While it's often considered taboo to talk about death and finances, they are both critical components of life that cannot be ignored. In order to be the triathlete of financial fitness, you MUST have a will, power of attorney, and other estate planning documents in place.

The Will. A will is a legal declaration of a person's wishes regarding the disposal of his or her property or estate after death. Without one, your assets may get tied up in probate for years, creating a legal nightmare for your survivors. It's also used to name guardians for minor children in the event of your untimely death. I hate to think about not being around, but this is one of the most important legal documents I have created. It brings me comfort knowing my family will be provided for in the event of my untimely demise.

Medical Directive. This document sets out the level and extent of care you want to receive if you become ill or incapacitated. For example, it tells your family if you want to be placed on life support or not. Think about what you want then create a medical directive.

Power of Attorney. While this can get a little complex, in essence, a power of attorney gives a designee the right to make legal decisions regarding your health and finances. You really need one in case you become ill or incapacitated, but you definitely want to learn more about the types and purposes of each. Do some research to learn more.

Revocable Trust. This document allows control over your estate. Again, there are different types, but the advantage is that it keeps your family members out of court, fighting in probate over your assets.

As you can see, the issues associated with these documents are pretty weighty but necessary. If you are missing any of these, it's time to get them in place and stored in a safe location.

Step 1: Find an organization or contact a lawyer to discuss your options.

_____

_____

Step 2: Get these legal documents created within three months or ASAP.

_____

_____

Step 3: Store these documents in safe locations that are accessible by a trustworthy person.

_____

_____

If you're a parent, this step is critical. If not, it's great information for any child you have in your life – grandkids, nieces, nephews, cousins, etc.

Oftentimes people's love for children leads them to make purchases they probably should have said "no" to. The last minute impulse buy, the "you've done a great job" snack, or the "stop this meltdown and I'll buy you something" toy that almost every adult has made (although it's not a great way to teach a lesson), often results in buyer's remorse later. The best way to avoid this situation, while helping kids take part in your financial fitness journey, is to take the time to teach them about money. They'll thank you for the lessons later.

Money Lesson 1: Income vs. Expenses

Children need to know that income is used to pay expenses. They should learn about earned income, or money you work for, and passive income, or money that works for you. They need to understand that expenses should not be higher than income if you want to be financially secure. Let them know that right now you are on a path to financial fitness and it would help a lot if they would keep that in mind the next time they ask for something.

Money Lesson 2: Needs vs. Wants

Everyone has needs that don't always match their wants. Kids must understand the difference between the two and how to prioritize needs over wants. They should learn how to pay for all of their necessities before they pay for the latest video game or pair of shoes. If they don't have enough income to pay for their needs, they must earn more to afford what they want. This lesson can be used to help reduce the frequency of their unnecessary requests so that you don't have to break their heart so often. Find ways to turn the lesson into a challenge to see how long the family can go without whining over non-essentials.

While there are many more money lessons kids need to learn, those two are the fundamentals. They are also critical if making your financial fitness regimen a family affair. Please don't feel like you have to shield kids from the reality of your financial situation. If they know that you are stressed about cash, they should know that you are doing something about it.

If they think that everything is OK and see that you are living a life you truly can't afford, they'll think they can spend freely without consequences as well. Not the best way to set your kids up for success.

Think about questions your kids may ask or how you will involve them in your financial fitness program. Just as if they would start exercising with you or eating healthier meals if you were on a physical fitness plan, they should be just as involved in your financial fitness journey.

DAY 28 | Reward Yourself

Being on a financial fitness plan can seem daunting at times. You may temporarily lose sight of the end goal and may get overwhelmed at the constant budgeting and saving that is required to achieve financial freedom. Trust me, I've been there. Because of that, it is extremely important to find ways to reward yourself throughout this journey.

Spending tons of money is not necessary to give yourself a reward. That's counterproductive. It's like giving yourself pizza, wings, and cake when you lose 30 pounds. Not the best idea. Instead, giving yourself rewards can be as simple as having coffee with a friend, taking a day off from work to relax at the beach, enjoying a day of rest reading a great book, or buying something inexpensive that you've set your sights on and saved for in the appropriate sinking fund.

All of this is to say that as with any journey requiring perseverance, it's important to maintain balance to make sure your success is long lasting. You have made some serious steps in the right direction, so now it's time to make a plan to keep yourself motivated going forward.

Think of each reward as a checkpoint that you cross on the road to financial fitness. Answer the questions below to plan a reward system that will keep you motivated:

1. What motivates you to be successful?

2. What do you like to do?

3. What do you like to receive?

4. Where would you like to go on vacation?

5. If you had an extra $50 to spend on something you want, what would you spend it on?

6. Who would you like to spend the day with?

7. What activity relaxes you?

8. What makes you feel powerful?

9. What is it that you want most in life?

Now take the answers to those questions and brainstorm checkpoint for rewards you can put in place to celebrate yourself as you become financially free.

Write your first goal/checkpoint below:

1. What is your first checkpoint?

_____

2. What would you like as a reward for reaching that checkpoint?

_____

Like any other goal you set out to accomplish, once you reach the summit, it's time to reflect, stay the course, and elevate yourself to the next level. Now that you have completed four weeks, or 28 days of financial fitness, you are well on your way to a lifetime of happiness and wealth.

Studies show that it takes 21 days to start a new habit. Because you have been engaged in your financial journey this long, staying on top of everything should be routine. Take a deep breath. Your financial situation is looking brighter. But don't rest. It's important to stay vigilant with your cash.

Have you ever wanted to lose weight, lost it, and eventually gained it back? If not, do you know someone who did? It's not that they wanted to get unhealthy, they just got comfortable and stopped monitoring themselves. I can share countless examples of that. Many of them featuring myself.

Take it from me, don't be that person. Choose a day each week to check your bank accounts. Choose a day each month to make your budget. Choose a time of the year to set new financial goals and remind yourself daily of how wonderful you are. Check in with your village regularly and choose to stay abreast of financial news by reading a book or magazine every few weeks. You'll be happy you did.

Use the space below to plan your financial to-dos so that you will know what to expect and when:

Day to check bank accounts: _____

Day of the month to create budget: _____

Time to set yearly financial goals: _____

Village check-in frequency: _____

Magazine to subscribe to: _____

Book to read: _____

Other: _____

Other: _____

Other: _____

Wow! You did it! Taking the steps to change your life can be a mix of exciting, scary, overwhelming, and daunting at times, but in almost every situation, it's worth it!

By now you are well on your way to better manage your money, stick to a budget, and get or maintain excellent credit. But like any major endeavor, taking these first steps is only the beginning. To make a lasting change, you must commit to stay fit.

Just like getting physically healthy, if you tone up and slim down by making temporary changes, eventually old habits resurface, and you go right back to where you began. Sometimes even worse! I don't want that to happen to you. The work you have done is commendable and worth preserving. So, follow the steps below and commit to stay financially fit now and forever.

1. What have you learned over the past 30 days?

2. What changes are you most proud of?

3. What word describes where you were when you started?

4. What word describes where you are right now?

5. Think of one thing you can refer back to when you start feeling overwhelmed or want to return to old spending habits?

6. What is one obstacle that may derail your progress?

7. How can you handle that obstacle should it arise?

8. Why do you want to get and stay financially fit?

Congratulations, you did it!
Financial freedom, here you come!

Reflections

Use this page for notes, to reflect, to doodle, share your thoughts, dreams, hopes, aspirations, and success about your journey to financial freedom. This is your safe space. Enjoy!

Book Club and Smart Money Village Discussion Questions

The following questions are designed to help people talk about money and communicate in a positive way. Now more than ever people need to be open and willing to share information to help each other succeed.

Discuss these questions with honesty, integrity, and an open-mind. Together, we can all do better.

1. What are your biggest money fears? Why?

2. What were you taught about money growing up?

3. What do you wish you had learned to help you have a better financial future?

4. What would you tell an 18-year old seeking to build a solid financial foundation?

5. Who is your money mentor?

6. If you could ask one person about personal finance, who would it be and why?

7. Do you think your financial future looks brighter than it did before reading this book? Explain.

8. How will you help others build a solid financial future?

9. What are you most proud of, financially speaking?

10. What do you want to be your legacy when it comes to personal finance?

Appendix

Glossary of Financial Terms

1. **401K** A qualified retirement plan that allows eligible employees of a company to save and invest for their own retirement on a tax deferred basis.

2. **403B** A retirement savings plan available to employees of certain public education organizations, non-profit employers, and cooperative hospital service organizations as well as to self-employed ministers.

3. **Bankruptcy** The legal proceeding involving a person or business that is unable to repay outstanding debts.

4. **Baseline** A minimum or starting point used for comparisons.

5. **Budget** An estimate of income and expenditure for a set period of time.

6. **Credit** The ability of a customer to obtain goods or services before payment, based on the trust that payment will be made in the future.

7. **Credit card** A small plastic card issued by a bank or business, allowing the holder to purchase goods or services on credit.

8. **Credit report** A detailed breakdown of an individual's credit history prepared by a credit bureau. Credit bureaus collect financial information about individuals and create credit reports based on that information, and lenders use the reports along with other details to determine loan applicants' creditworthiness.

9. **Credit score** A statistical number that evaluates a consumer's creditworthiness and is based on credit history. It ranges from 300 to 850, and the higher the score, the more financially trustworthy a person is considered to be.

10. **Debt** Something, typically money, that is owed or due.

11. **Debt load** The total amount of debt that a company or person is carrying.

12. **Earned income** Money derived or earned from paid work.

13. **Expenses** The cost required for something; the money spent on something.

14. **Financial barriers** Situations that make it difficult to afford items.

15. **Financial fitness** Living in a way that does not exceed income earned or put financial strain on savings goals.

16. **Financial literacy** Education and understanding of various financial areas, including topics related to managing personal finance, money, and investing.

17. **Foreclosure**   The action of taking possession of a mortgaged property. when the mortgagor fails to keep up their mortgage payments.

18. **Income**   Money received, especially on a regular basis, for work or through investments.

19. **Interest**   Money paid regularly at a particular rate for the use of money lent.

20. **IRA**   Individual Retirement Account; a retirement savings account in which income taxes on certain deposits and on all gains are deferred until withdrawals are made

21. **Passive income**   Passive income is income that requires little to no effort to earn and maintain. It is frequently received through investments and other automatic income streams.

22. **Personal finance**   The management of money and financial decisions for a person or family including budgeting, investments, retirement planning and investments.

23. **Retirement**   The withdrawal from one's position or occupation or from one's active working life.

24. **ROTH IRA**   A tax-advantaged, retirement savings account that allows you to withdraw your savings tax-free after the age of 59 ½.

25. **Savings hack**   Tricks and tips that help people save money.

26. **Sinking fund**   A fund formed by periodically setting aside money for the gradual repayment of a debt or replacement of a wasting asset.

27. **Tax Refund**   The difference between taxes paid and taxes owed.

28. **W-4**   An Internal Revenue Service (IRS) tax form completed by an employee in the United States to indicate their tax situation (exemptions, status, etc.) to the employer.

29. **Wealth**   The state of being rich; material prosperity

How to pay off consumer debt using the simple debt reduction method

Sample debt:

Credit Card 1	5% Interest Rate	$500 Balance Due
Credit Card 2	10% Interest Rate	$1500 Balance Due
Personal Loan	3% Interest Rate	$700 Balance Due

The smallest debt is credit card 1. Do not worry about the interest rate. Pay the minimum balance on the other debts and pay as much as possible on the credit card.

When done paying off the $500 for credit card 1, take the money you were paying on credit card 1 and add that to the personal loan since that is the next smallest debt.

Once the personal loan is paid off, take all of your money and pay off the last debt, credit card 2.

That's it! Works like a charm.

Made in United States
Orlando, FL
17 April 2023

32188284R00039